The Mathematics of Buying
Mathematics for Everyday Living

Ron Larson
Robert P. Hostetler

Exercises prepared with the assistance of
David E. Heyd

Updated and revised by
Marjorie J. Bertram

meridian
A DIVISION OF LARSON TEXTS, INC.

**This book is published by
Meridian Creative Group, a Division of Larson Texts, Inc.**

(800) 530-2355
http://www.meridiancg.com

Printed in the United States of America

International Standard Book Number: 1-887050-21-3

10 9 8 7 6 5 4 3

Preface

Mathematics for Everyday Living is a series of workbooks designed to give students a solid and practical grasp of the mathematics used in daily life.

Each workbook in the series features practical consumer information, solved examples, and "Try one!" exercises with which students can use a particular skill immediately following its introduction. Complete solutions to the "Try one!" exercises are provided in the back of the workbook along with answers to odd-numbered exercises.

The workbook, "*The Mathematics of Buying*," is divided into five sections, each of which address a set of mathematic skills and concepts that enable students to become wise consumers.

- In the first section, "Unit Prices," students will learn how savings can be realized by the consumer on a daily basis simply by understanding comparison shopping.

- In section two, "Markup," students will learn the mathematics behind the setting of retail selling prices.

- Section three, "Discounts," teaches students the practical skills necessary to determine when advertised discounts are truly bargains.

- In section four, "Utility Bills," calculation of telephone, long-distance, gas and electric bills is taught. Ways in which the consumer can save money and energy are discussed.

- Section five presents a career spotlight. Description of a career in pharmaceuticals includes educational requirements, potential income, job highlights and an outlook for employment. Also provided is a comprehensive set of review exercises from the first four sections. Exercises in this section are presented within the context of a career in pharmaceuticals.

Instructors may download a Teacher's Recource Guide for this title on our website (http://home.meridiancg.com/mfelpdf.html).

Finally, a "Thank-you" is owed to Richard, John, Michele, Linda, and especially Cheryl, all of whom helped make this project go as smoothly as it has.

Marjorie J. Bertram

Contents

Section 1
Unit Prices

Most consumers spend a great deal of time shopping for major purchases such as houses, cars, furniture, and appliances. They want to get the most for their money, and they know that by comparing prices they may be able to save several hundred dollars in a single purchase. Surprisingly, many of these same people spend very little time comparing prices for day-to-day items that differ by only a few cents. Yet taken over a year's time, such items can provide substantial savings for a conscientious shopper. To illustrate this point, we compared the prices of some common items in a local supermarket. The results of this survey are shown in Table 1.

TABLE 1

Variations in Unit Prices

Item	Number of Choices	Year's Supply*	Least Costly		Moderately Costly		Most Costly	
			Unit Price	*Annual Cost*	*Unit Price*	*Annual Cost*	*Unit Price*	*Annual Cost*
Peanut butter	25	12 lb	8.80¢ per oz	$16.90	10.50¢ per oz	$20.16	12.50¢ per oz	$24.00
Laundry soap	34	128 lb	8.95¢ per oz	$183.30	9.72¢ per oz	$199.07	12.79¢ per oz	$261.94
Toothpaste	24	10 lb	26.41¢ per oz	$42.26	35.78¢ per oz	$57.25	47.46¢ per oz	$75.94
Dry dog food	38	480 lb	27.20¢ per lb	$130.56	35.20¢ per lb	$168.96	62.40¢ per lb	$299.52
		Total		**$373.02**		**$445.44**		**$661.40**

*Estimated for a family of four

Table 1 suggests three important points for shoppers.

1) When shopping for a particular item, a consumer may be faced with literally dozens of different brands and sizes from which to choose.

2) Differences in a few cents per item can add up to differences in hundreds of dollars over a year's time.

3) The most useful comparison between prices is the **unit price**. The unit price of an item is defined as the ratio of the **total price** of the item to the number of units (**total units**) of the item (ounces, pounds, etc.).

$$\text{Unit Price} = \frac{\text{Total Price}}{\text{Total Units}}$$

If the units of an item are mixed (such as 5 lb, 4 oz) we must convert to a single unit of measure before finding the unit price. For example, if pounds is the desired unit, 5 lb, 4 oz should be converted to 5.25 lb, and if ounces is the desired unit, 5 lb, 4 oz should be converted to 84 oz as demonstrated in Examples 1–3.

EXAMPLE 1   Finding the unit price

Find the unit price (per ounce) for a 12-ounce jar of strawberry jam that costs $2.09.

SOLUTION

The unit price (per ounce) is

$$\text{Unit Price} = \frac{\text{Total Price}}{\text{Total Units}} = \frac{\$2.09}{12 \text{ oz}}$$

$$\approx \$0.1742 \text{ per ounce}$$

$$= 17.42\text{¢ per ounce.} \qquad \blacklozenge$$

EXAMPLE 2   Finding the unit price

Find the unit price (per ounce) for a 4.6-ounce tube of tooth-paste that costs $1.89.

SOLUTION

The unit price (per ounce) is

$$\text{Unit Price} = \frac{\text{Total Price}}{\text{Total Units}} = \frac{\$1.89}{4.6 \text{ oz}}$$

$$\approx \$0.4109 \text{ per ounce}$$

$$= 41.09\cancel{c} \text{ per ounce.} \qquad \blacklozenge$$

EXAMPLE 3   Finding the unit price

Find the unit price (per ounce) for a 2-pound, 7-ounce box of detergent for $3.79.

SOLUTION

Since the weight of this item is given in pounds *and* ounces, we first convert to ounces by using the conversion factor 1 pound = 16 ounces. Thus, the total number of ounces is

$$\text{Total Ounces} = 2 \text{ lb} + 7 \text{ oz} = 32 \text{ oz} + 7 \text{ oz} = 39 \text{ oz.}$$

Finally, the unit price (per ounce) is

$$\text{Unit Price} = \frac{\text{Total Price}}{\text{Total Units}} = \frac{\$3.79}{39 \text{ oz}}$$

$$\approx \$0.0972 \text{ per ounce}$$

$$= 9.72\cancel{c} \text{ per ounce.} \qquad \blacklozenge$$

Try one!

Find the unit price (per ounce) of a 3-pound, 8-ounce container of fresh mushrooms for $8.82.

Answer: _____

EXAMPLE 4 **Comparing unit prices**

Which is the better bargain, a 9-ounce box of breakfast cereal for $2.49 or a 13-ounce box of the same cereal for $3.49?

SOLUTION

The unit price for the smaller box is

$$\text{Unit Price} = \frac{\text{Total Price}}{\text{Total Units}} = \frac{\$2.49}{9 \text{ oz}}$$

$$\approx \$0.2767 \text{ per ounce}$$

$$= 27.67\cent \text{ per ounce.}$$

The unit price for the larger box is

$$\text{Unit Price} = \frac{\text{Total Price}}{\text{Total Units}} = \frac{\$3.49}{13 \text{ oz}}$$

$$\approx \$0.2685 \text{ per ounce}$$

$$= 26.85\text{¢ per ounce}$$

Thus, the larger box has a slightly smaller unit price and it is the better bargain. ◆

Try one!

Which is the better bargain? A 32-ounce carton of chocolate milk for $1.69 or a 64-ounce carton of the same brand of chocolate milk for $2.79?

Answer: _____

EXAMPLE 5 Finding the unit price for multiple quantities

Which is the better bargain, three 12-ounce cans of corn for $2.07 or two 16-ounce cans for $1.89?

SOLUTION

Since there is a total of 36 ounces in the three 12-ounce cans, their unit price is

$$\text{Unit Price} = \frac{\text{Total Price}}{\text{Total Units}} = \frac{\$2.07}{36 \text{ oz}}$$

$$= \$0.0575 \text{ per ounce}$$

$$= 5.75 \text{¢ per ounce.}$$

Similarly, there is a total of 32 ounces in the two 16-ounce cans, which implies that their unit price is

$$\text{Unit Price} = \frac{\text{Total Price}}{\text{Total Units}} = \frac{\$1.89}{32 \text{ oz}}$$

$$\approx \$0.0591 \text{ per ounce}$$

$$= 5.91 \text{¢ per ounce.}$$

Thus, the smaller cans are the better bargain. ◆

In most instances, smaller quantities of a particular product have higher unit prices than larger quantities. This is mainly due to the cost of packaging. Several small packages generally cost more to produce than one larger package that holds an equivalent amount. One should not assume, however, that the unit price is always less for larger quantities. For instance, in Example 4, the larger container was the better buy, but in Example 5, the smaller container was the better buy.

Try one!

Which is the better bargain, two 12.5-ounce bottles of real maple syrup for $8.38, or six 4-ounce bottles for $9.54?

Answer: _____

EXAMPLE 6   Using the unit cost to find the annual cost

Tom Hendricks' doctor has prescribed two 250 mg capsules of a certain medication every day to control his allergy. If prescribed under the brand name, the capsules cost $25.54 per 100 and if prescribed under the generic name they cost $18.24 per 100. Tom's pharmacist told him that both names are equally effective. How much would Tom save in a year by buying the generic-name capsules?

SOLUTION

For the brand-name capsules, the unit price is

$$\text{Unit Price} = \frac{\text{Total Price}}{\text{Total Units}} = \frac{\$25.54}{100 \text{ cap}}$$

$$= \$0.2554 \text{ per capsule.}$$

Taking two capsules per day, a year's supply would cost

$$\text{Annual Cost} = (365)(2)(\$0.2554) \approx \$186.44.$$

Under the generic name, the unit price is

$$\text{Unit Price} = \frac{\text{Total Price}}{\text{Total Units}} = \frac{\$18.24}{100 \text{ cap}}$$

$$= \$0.1824 \text{ per capsule,}$$

and a year's supply would cost

$$\text{Annual Cost} = (365)(2)(\$0.1824) \approx \$133.15.$$

Therefore, by buying the generic-name capsules, Tom would save

$$\$186.44 - \$133.15 = \$53.29. \qquad \blacklozenge$$

Try one!

Jim Miller has an average of three cups of tea per day, using one teabag per cup. He purchases name brand teabags in boxes of 100 bags for $2.89. Recently he tried the store brand tea bags, found that they were comparable in quality, and decided to switch brands. If the storebrand costs $2.09 for 100 tea bags, how much will Jim save per year?

Answer: _____

Some products are packaged in containers identified by different units. For instance, ice cream can be purchased in pint, quart, half-gallon, or gallon containers. To compare prices involving different units, it is necessary to first convert to a common unit. Table 2 lists some common units together with their **conversion factors**.

TABLE 2

Conversion Factors For Common Units of Weight and Measure*

Weights: pound (lb), ounce (oz), gram (g), kilogram (kg)

1 lb	16 oz	453.6 g	0.4536 kg
1 oz	0.0625 lb	28.35 g	0.02835 kg
1 g	0.001 kg	0.002205 lb	0.03527 kg
1 kg	1000 g	2.205 lb	35.27 oz

Measures: gallon (gal), quart (qt), pint (pt), ounce (oz), liter (L), milliliter (mL)

1 gal	4 qt	8 pt	128 oz	3.785 L	3785 mL
1 qt	0.25 gal	2 pt	32 oz	0.9463 L	946.3 mL
1 pt	0.125 gal	0.5 qt	16 oz	0.4732 L	473.2 mL
1 oz	29.57 mL	0.03125 qt	0.0625 pt	0.02957 L	0.0078 gal
1 L	1000 mL	0.2642 gal	1.057 qt	2.114 pt	33.82 oz
1 mL	0.001 L	0.0002642 gal	0.002114 pt	0.001057 qt	0.03382 oz

*Conversions between metric and English systems are approximations.

EXAMPLE 7   **Finding common units for comparison**

A certain brand of ice cream costs $1.79 for a pint and $4.59 for a half-gallon. Which is the more economical way to buy this brand of ice cream?

SOLUTION

If we choose the pint as the basic unit of comparison, the unit price for the smaller container is

$$\text{Unit Price} = \frac{\text{Total Price}}{\text{Total Units}} = \frac{\$1.79}{1 \text{ pt}}$$

$$= \$1.79 \text{ per pint}.$$

For the larger container, we note that the conversion factor from gallons to pints is 1 gallon = 8 pints. Therefore, the total units in the larger container is

$$\text{Total Units} = \left(\tfrac{1}{2}\right)(1 \text{ gal}) = \left(\tfrac{1}{2}\right)(8 \text{ pt}) = 4 \text{ pints},$$

and the unit price for the larger container is

$$\text{Unit Price} = \frac{\text{Total Price}}{\text{Total Units}} = \frac{\$4.59}{4 \text{ pt}}$$

$$= \$1.1475 \text{ per pint}$$

$$\approx \$1.15 \text{ per pint}.$$

Hence, the half-gallon container is more economical.   ◆

Note in Example 7 that we did not have to choose the pint as the common unit of comparison. We could just as easily have chosen the quart, gallon, or in this particular case, the half-gallon would have been convenient.

Try one!

A certain brand of quick rice costs $3.29 for a 1-pound, 12-ounce box and $1.99 for a 14-ounce box. Which is the more economical way to purchase this rice?

Answer: _____

EXAMPLE 8   **Finding common units for comparison**

Chef Wagner's favorite brand of imported olive oil is available in four sizes: a) 3 liters for $22.15, b) 500 milliliters for $5.75, c) 2.114 pints for $10.39, d) 8.45 ounces for $3.79. Which of these sizes has the smallest unit price?

SOLUTION

If we choose the liter as the unit of comparison, the unit prices are as follows:

a. Unit Price $= \dfrac{\text{Total Price}}{\text{Total Units}} = \dfrac{\$22.15}{3 \text{ L}}$

$\approx \$7.38$ per liter

b. Total Units $= 500 \text{ ml} = 500(0.001 \text{ L}) = 0.5 \text{ L}$

Unit Price $= \dfrac{\text{Total Price}}{\text{Total Units}} = \dfrac{\$5.75}{0.5 \text{ L}}$

$= \$11.50$ per liter

c. Total Units $= 2.114 \text{ pt} \approx 1 \text{ L}$

Unit Price $= \dfrac{\text{Total Price}}{\text{Total Units}} \approx \dfrac{\$10.39}{1 \text{ L}}$

$= \$10.39$ per liter

d. Total Units $= 8.45 \text{ oz} \approx (8.45)(0.02957 \text{ L}) \approx 0.2499 \text{ L}$

Unit Price $= \dfrac{\text{Total Price}}{\text{Total Units}} = \dfrac{\$3.79}{0.2499 \text{ L}}$

$\approx \$15.17$ per liter

Consequently, the 3-liter size has the smallest unit price. ◆

Try one!

Which of the following sizes of soda-pop has the smaller unit price: a 2-liter bottle for $1.59 or a 20-ounce bottle for 79¢?

Answer: _____

EXAMPLE 9   **Finding common units for comparison**

Fred and Marlene Wong are driving from the United States to Canada. Before leaving, they fill their car with gasoline at the rate of $1.249 per gallon. The first time they stop to buy gasoline in Canada, they are startled to find the price is $1.419 (U.S. dollars) per gallon. After complaining to the station attendant, the attendant tells Fred and Marlene that a Canadian gallon is larger than a U.S. gallon. If 1 Canadian gallon is approximately equal to 1.201 U.S. gallons, which gasoline was cheaper?

SOLUTION

For the gasoline purchased in the United States, the unit price is $1.249 per gallon (U.S.). For the gasoline purchased in Canada, the unit price is

$$\text{Unit Price} = \frac{\text{Total Price}}{\text{Total Units}} = \frac{\$1.419}{1 \text{ gal (Can)}}$$

$$\approx \frac{\$1.419}{1.201 \text{ gal (U.S.)}}$$

$$\approx \$1.182 \text{ per gal (U.S.)}.$$

Therefore, the Canadian gasoline was cheaper.   ◆

As a final comment, we should point out that the unit price should not be the only criterion used to decide which purchase to make. In some instances, price serves as a measure of product quality. Higher prices may mean better quality; however, we encourage consumers to try the less expensive brands to see if the quality is indeed lower and if this difference is sufficient to offset the savings in cost. Remember that the term "brand-name" is synonymous with "highly advertised product." It costs money to advertise, and the higher price of a brand-name product may represent nothing more than the additional cost of advertising. Manufacturers would like consumers to believe that "shoppers get what they pay for," indicating that expensive products are necessarily better than cheaper products. A smart shopper is willing to keep an open mind and consider switching to less familiar brands.   ◆

Important Terms

Conversion Factor

Total Price

Total Units

Unit Price

Important Formulas

$$\text{Unit Price} = \frac{\text{Total Price}}{\text{Total Units}}$$

CONSUMER HINTS

- Take a hand-held calculator with you when you do major shopping. When you find items with smaller unit prices than those you usually purchase, consider switching. If you find the less expensive item suits your needs, you have saved yourself some money.

- Most large supermarkets have their own brands and some carry generic products with no brand names. These items usually have smaller unit prices than nationally advertised brands.

- Although larger sizes usually have smaller unit prices, this is not necessarily the case. The "large economy size" may turn out to have a higher price than the regular size.

- Be sure to use the same unit of weight or measure when comparing unit prices.

- Staple items (items you use in large quantities) have the greatest potential for annual savings. Therefore, the more you use of a product, the more conscious you should be of its unit price.

SECTION 1   EXERCISES

In Exercises 1–3, find the unit price per ounce for each of the following items. Where conversions are necessary, use Table 2 on page 9.

1. A 32-ounce jar of grape jelly for $1.98.

Answer: _____

2. A 27-ounce can of orange drink for $1.17.

Answer: _____

3. A 115-ounce box of detergent for $5.22.

Answer: _____

In Exercises 4–6, find the unit price per pound for each of the following items.

4. A 5-lb bag of sugar for $2.19.

Answer: _____

5. A 28-ounce package of instant potatoes for $3.15.

Answer: _____

6. A 25-pound bag of flour for $8.45.

Answer: _____

In Exercises 7–9, find the unit price per quart for each of the following items.

7. A 24-quart case of motor oil for $26.16.

Answer: _____

8. A gallon of paint for $19.95.

Answer: _____

9. A liter of paint for $4.14.

Answer: _____

In Exercises 10–12, find the unit price per liter for each of the following items.

10. A 2-liter bottle of soft drink for $1.29.

Answer: _____

11. A quart of oil for $1.59.

Answer: _____

12. A gallon of windshield washer fluid for $1.29.

Answer: _____

In Exercises 13–26, find the unit price for each container size and determine which is the better buy. Assume in each case that the product in each container is of the same quality.

13. A 10-pound sack of potatoes for $2.79 or a 5-pound sack for $1.59.

Answer: _____

14. One gallon of milk for $2.50 or 2 quarts for $1.30. (List units in dollars per quart.)

Answer: _____

15. A 16-ounce can of orange juice concentrate for $1.89, a 12-ounce can for $1.39, or a 6-ounce can for $0.99.

Answer: _____

16. A 3-pound package of bacon for $8.29 or a 0.78-pound package for $2.18.

Answer: _____

17. One dollar and thirty-five cents for $1\frac{1}{4}$ pounds of peas or 89¢ for 10 ounces. (List units in dollars per ounce.)

Answer: _____

18. A pound of apples for $1.09 or a bushel (60 pounds) for $18.00.

Answer: _____

19. A 1.89-liter container of bleach for 79¢, 946 milliliters for 51¢, or 3.79 liters for $1.19. (List units in dollars per liter.)

Answer: _____

20. A 227-gram box of corn flakes for $1.40, 340 grams for $1.93, or 680 grams for $3.19.

Answer: _____

21. A 2-liter bottle of soft drink for $1.49 or an 8-pint pack for $2.19. (List units in dollars per ounce.)

Answer: _____

22. Two $25\frac{3}{4}$-ounce cans of vegetable beef soup for $4.95 or four $10\frac{3}{4}$-ounce cans for $4.20.

Answer: _____

23. A 5-pound bag of flour for $1.79, a 10-pound bag for $3.45, or a 25-pound bag for $8.45.

Answer: _____

24. Two 32-ounce jars of orange marmalade for $6.99 or a 2-pound jar for $4.75. (List units in dollars per pound.)

Answer: _____

25. A 5-gallon can of motor oil for $17.80 or a 24-quart case for $20.76.

Answer: _____

26. A 50-pound bag of lawn fertilizer for $19.40 or an 80-pound bag for $32.24.

Answer: _____

27. The James family uses an average of 3 gallons of milk a week. They can buy it at the grocery store for $2.50 per gallon when they do their regular shopping, or once a week they can make a special trip to a farm (4.5 miles one way) and purchase the milk for $2.33 per gallon.

    a. How much less would the James family spend a year on milk by buying the milk on the farm? (Ignore the cost of driving.)

Answer: _____

    b. If the price of gasoline is $1.379 per gallon and the James' car gets 18 miles per gallon, is there an actual savings in buying the milk at the farm?

Answer: _____

28. Carol and Philip Songer and their family use an average of 4 dozen eggs per week. If Carol buys them at the supermarket while doing regular shopping, the eggs average $1.09 per dozen for grade A large. Philip passes an egg distributor on his way home from work and there he can get grade B large eggs for 84¢ per dozen. How much would the Songers save in a year by purchasing the eggs from the distributor?

Answer: _____

29. Tom and Joyce Nickels use 30 pounds of coffee in a year. They have been buying coffee in 1-pound cans that cost $3.59. How much would they save in a year by buying their coffee in 3-pound cans that cost $10.25?

Answer: _____

30. George Miller buys a bag of chips every day from a vending machine for 60¢ per bag. How much would he save in a year by buying packages of 9 bags for $2.79 instead? (Assume there are 365 days in a year.)

Answer: _____

Section **2**
Markup

In Section 1, we discussed one way for consumers to save money on purchases by comparing unit prices in order to decide what to buy. A second way to save on purchases is by deciding where to buy. We have all had the experience of buying an item at one store and later finding that we could have paid less for the identical item at another store. The basic reason for this difference is **markup**. Markup is the difference between the amount a retailer pays for an item and the price at which the retailer sells the item to the consumer.

By defining **cost** as the amount a retailer pays for an item, we obtain the following equation:

Selling Price = Cost + Markup.

Symbolically, we denote this equation by

$S = C + M.$

This equation suggests that we can find the selling price if we are given the cost and the markup. Using algebra we can juggle the equation around in order to determine any one of the three quantities (markup, selling price, or cost) by knowing the other two.

Find Selling Price (given cost and markup):

$$S = C + M$$

Find Markup (given selling price and cost):

$$M = S - C$$

Find Cost (given selling price and markup):

$$C = S - M$$

EXAMPLE 1   Finding markup

A sports store pays $90.00 for a pair of ski boots and sells them for $149.00. What is the markup?

SOLUTION

We are given $S = \$149.00$ and $C = \$90.00$. Therefore, the markup is

$$M = S - C = \$149.00 - \$90.00 = \$59.00.$$ ◆

Try one!

A jeweler pays $650.00 for a diamond and sells it for $1,040.00. How much is the markup?

Answer: _____

EXAMPLE 2   Finding selling price

An automobile dealer pays $16,500.00 for a car and sells it with a markup of $1,560.00. What is the selling price?

SOLUTION

We are given C = $16,500.00 and M = $1,560.00. Therefore, the selling price is

$$S = C + M = \$16,500.00 + \$1,560.00 = \$18,060.00. \blacklozenge$$

Try one!

A pair of cowboy boots cost a shoe store $125.00 and there is a markup of $54.95. What is the selling price?

Answer: _____

EXAMPLE 3   Finding cost

A jeweler sells a ring for $450.00. If the ring has a markup of $240.00, what is the jeweler's cost?

SOLUTION

We are given S = $450.00 and M = $240.00. Therefore, the cost is

$$C = S - M = \$450.00 - \$240.00 = \$210.00. \qquad \blacklozenge$$

Try one!

A truck dealership advertises a pick-up truck for $22,495.00. If the markup on this truck is $2,137.00, what is the dealer's cost?

Answer: _____

How large should the markup on an item be? Is $23.00 a fair markup, is $100.00 too much, is 50¢ too little? Obviously, the answer depends upon the cost of the item being sold. A markup of $23.00 is outrageously high on an item that costs $5.00, but is a reasonable markup on an item that costs $100.00. Since the dollar value of a markup tells little by itself, we usually express markup as a rate (or percentage), based on either the cost or the selling price.

As a rate based on the cost, we have

$$\textbf{Markup Rate on Cost} = R = \frac{M}{C} = \frac{\text{Markup}}{\text{Cost}}.$$

As a rate based on the selling price, we have

$$\textbf{Markup Rate on Selling Price} = r = \frac{M}{S} = \frac{\text{Markup}}{\text{Selling Price}}.$$

EXAMPLE 4   Finding the markup rate

Find the markup rate based on cost and selling price for the three items listed in Examples 1–3.

	Item	C	M	S
a.	Ski boots	$90.00	$59.00	$149.00
b.	Car	$16,500.00	$1,560.00	$18,060.00
c.	Ring	$210.00	$240.00	$450.00

SOLUTION

a. For the ski boots, we have

$$R = \frac{M}{C} = \frac{\$59.00}{\$90.00} \approx 0.6556 \approx 65.6\%,$$

$$r = \frac{M}{S} = \frac{\$59.00}{\$149.00} \approx 0.3960 = 39.6\%.$$

b. For the car, we have

$$R = \frac{M}{C} = \frac{\$1,560.00}{\$16,500.00} \approx 0.0945 \approx 9.5\%,$$

$$r = \frac{M}{S} = \frac{\$1,560.00}{\$18,060.00} \approx 0.0864 \approx 8.6\%.$$

c. For the ring, we have

$$R = \frac{M}{C} = \frac{\$240.00}{\$210.00} \approx 1.1429 \approx 114.3\%,$$

$$r = \frac{M}{S} = \frac{\$240.00}{\$450.00} \approx 0.5333 \approx 53.3\%.$$

◆

Try one!

Find the markup rate based on cost R and the markup rate based on selling price r for a pair of cowboy boots that cost the shoe store \$125.00 and have a markup of \$54.95.

Answer: _____

Answer: _____

From Example 4 we can observe that markup rates can differ greatly from one item to another. For instance, there is usually a much higher markup rate on jewelry and clothing than there is on automobiles and groceries. Additionally, it can be noted that for a given value of M, R is always larger than r. When markup rates are quoted by retailers to their customers, the rates are usually based on selling price. ◆

Distinct from Examples 1–4, there is another type of markup problem that is of interest to consumers. In this situation, the markup rate is known along with either the cost or the selling price, but not both. For instance, suppose the markup rate and selling price of an item are known. How can the retailer's cost be determined? Or, suppose the markup rate and cost are known. How can the selling price be determined? The solutions to these problems depend upon the base on which the markup rate is calculated. If the markup rate, R, based on cost and the selling price, S, are known, then the equation for the cost is

$$C = \frac{S}{1 + R}.$$

This formula can be derived in the following way:

Since we know that $R = \frac{M}{C}$, we can say that $RC = M$.
Since $S = C + M$ (or equivilently $C + M = S$), we have

$C + M = S$	**Given**
$C + RC = S$	**Substitution of RC for M**
$C(1 + R) = S$	**Distributive property**
$C = \dfrac{S}{1 + R}.$	**Division property**

In a similar way, we can show that the equation for the selling price is

$$S = \frac{C}{1 - r}. \qquad\qquad\qquad \blacklozenge$$

Table 3 provides a summary of the formulas for markup on cost and markup on selling price.

TABLE 3

Summary of Formulas for Markup

Markup on Cost	Markup on Selling Price
$R = \dfrac{M}{C}$	$r = \dfrac{M}{S}$
$M = RC$	$M = rS$
$C = \dfrac{S}{1 + R}$	$S = \dfrac{C}{1 - r}$

| EXAMPLE 5 | Finding the selling price given the markup rate |

Pat Stoner began work at a small clothing store and was asked to help price some new items. The manager told Pat to mark the items up 40%. Pat understood this to mean 40% of the cost, but the manager meant 40% of the selling price. The error was not discovered until after the sale of a pair of jeans which cost the store $24.00. Was Pat's error in favor of the customer or the store?

SOLUTION

Assuming the 40% to be based on cost, we have $R = 40\%$ $= 0.40$ and $C = \$24.00$. Therefore, Pat's markup was

$$M = RC = (0.40)(\$24.00) = \$9.60,$$

and the selling price of the pair of jeans was

$$S = C + M = \$24.00 + \$9.60 = \$33.60.$$

Assuming that the 40% is to be based on the selling price, we have $r = 40\% = 0.40$. The selling price is

$$S = \frac{C}{1 - r} = \frac{\$24.00}{1 - 0.40}$$

$$= \frac{\$24.00}{0.60}$$

$$= \$40.00.$$

Since the difference between the two selling prices is

$$\$40.00 - \$33.60 = \$6.40,$$

the store sold the jeans for $6.40 less than the manager had intended. ◆

Try one!

a. The cost of a pair of running shoes is $47.70. If Pat Stoner is asked to mark this item up 40% based on selling price, what will the correct selling price be?

Answer: _____

b. If Pat Stoner mistakenly bases the 40% markup on cost, what will the markup be?

Answer: _____

EXAMPLE 6   Finding the cost given the selling price and markup rate

Find the cost to the retailer for a bicycle selling for $280.00 with a markup rate of 45% based on selling price.

SOLUTION

Since $S = \$280.00$ and $r = 45\% = 0.45$, we have

$$M = rS = (0.45)(\$280.00) = \$126.00,$$

and the cost to the retailer is

$$C = S - M = \$280.00 - \$126.00 = \$154.00. \qquad \blacklozenge$$

Try one!

Find the cost to the retailer for a car selling for $17,650.00 with a markup rate of 9% based on selling price.

Answer: _____

EXAMPLE 7	Finding the cost given the selling price and markup rate

Find the cost to the retailer for a man's suit selling for $349.00 with a markup rate of 180% based on cost.

SOLUTION

Since $S = \$349.00$ and $R = 180\% = 1.80$, we have

$$C = \frac{S}{1 + R} = \frac{\$349.00}{1 + 1.80}$$

$$= \frac{\$349.00}{2.80}$$

$$\approx \$124.64. \qquad \blacklozenge$$

Try one!

Find the cost to the retailer for a woman's suit selling for $219.95 with a markup rate of 130% based on cost.

Answer: _____

| EXAMPLE 8 | **Finding the cost given the selling price and markup rate** |

Find the cost to the retailer for a candy bar selling for 50¢ with a markup rate of 30% based on cost.

SOLUTION

Since $S = \$0.50$ and $R = 30\% = 0.30$, we have

$$C = \frac{S}{1 + R} = \frac{\$0.50}{1 + 0.30}$$

$$= \frac{\$0.50}{1.30}$$

$$\approx \$0.3846$$

$$\approx \$0.38. \qquad \blacklozenge$$

While it is true that the markup rate on retail items can be great, in fairness to retailers we should emphasize that markup is not the same as profit. Retailers have many expenses other than the cost of goods sold, and in order to make a profit, a retailer must charge a markup that will more than cover these expenses. Since many of these additional expenses are related to customer services, consumers who are hunting for lower markup rates should seek out retailers with minimal customer services. Some common customer services are:

Customer Service	**Expense to Retailer**
Heating or Air Conditioning	Utility Bills
Assistance by Sales Personnel	Salaries and Commissions
Charge Accounts	Bookkeeping Expenses
Wide Selection	Cost of Large Inventory
Attractive Surroundings	Decorating Costs
Convenient Parking	High Rent or Property Taxes
Delivery	Delivery Costs
Long Hours	Cost of Larger Sales Staff
Small Neighborhood Store	Fewer Sales

During the last several years, there has been a rapid growth in a new breed of stores that offer so-called "discount prices." Some of the more popular types are the discount department stores, factory outlets, catalog showrooms, and warehouse clubs. For the most part, these stores can offer lower prices because they offer fewer customer services and thus can afford to operate on a smaller markup per item. Furthermore, they hope to make up for their smaller profit per item by increased volume in sales as a result of their lower prices.

EXAMPLE 9   **Comparing markup rates**

George and Pam Dorchester are considering joining a warehouse shopping club that has a $35.00 annual membership fee. The warehouse stocks a selection of staple items such as canned goods, baking supplies, paper goods, fresh produce and frozen foods. The markup on these items is 20% based on cost. George and Pam estimate that their current annual grocery bill for staples is $2,000.00 at a supermarket whose markup is 40% based on cost. How much would George and Pam save by joining the warehouse?

SOLUTION

We begin by figuring the annual cost of the Dorchesters' staples. If $S = \$2,000.00$ and $R = 40\% = 0.40$, then the supermarket's cost for these staples is

$$C = \frac{S}{1 + R} = \frac{\$2,000.00}{1 + 0.40}$$

$$= \frac{\$2,000.00}{1.40}$$

$$\approx \$1,428.57.$$

If purchased at the warehouse, the markup rate would be $R = 20\% = 0.20$ and the markup would be

$$M = RC = (0.20)(\$1,428.57) \approx \$285.71.$$

Consequently, the selling price would be

$$S = C + M = \$1,428.57 + \$285.71 = \$1,714.28.$$

Adding the annual membership fee yields

$$\text{Annual Expense} = \$1,714.28 + \$35.00 = \$1,749.28.$$

Therefore, the Dorchesters' savings by joining the warehouse would be

$$\$2,000.00 - \$1,749.28 = \$250.72. \qquad \blacklozenge$$

Before concluding this section, we remind you that the formulas in this section can be derived from three basic equations:

$$S = C + M,$$

$$M = RC, \text{ and}$$

$$M = rS.$$

Using these three equations and a little bit of algebra, we can solve any of the examples in this section. For instance, in Example 7 the suit sells for \$349.00 with a markup rate of 180% based on cost. We are asked to find C given that $S = \$349.00$ and $R = 180\% = 1.8$. Since $S = C + M$ and $M = RC$, we have

$C + M = S$	**Given**
$C + RC = S$	**Substitution of RC for M**
$C + (1.8)C = \$349.00$	**$R = 1.8$ and $S = \$349.00$**
$C(1 + 1.8) = \$349.00$	**Distributive property**
$C = \dfrac{\$349.00}{1 + 1.8}$	**Divide both sides by $1 + 1.8$**
$C \approx \$124.64.$	

Important Terms

C, cost M, markup S, selling price

r, markup rate on selling price R, markup rate on cost

Important Formulas

$$M = S - C \qquad\qquad R = \frac{M}{C}$$

$$S = C + M \qquad\qquad r = \frac{M}{S}$$

$$C = S - M \qquad\qquad S = \frac{C}{1 - r}$$

$$M = RC \qquad\qquad C = \frac{S}{1 + R}$$

$$M = rS$$

CONSUMER HINTS

- Markup rates differ from store to store and from item to item. Comparing prices at different stores is time consuming, but it is the best way to end up with consistently low prices on your purchases.

- The two major factors in determining markup are volume and customer services. If you shop at a "no frills" store with a high volume, you should expect the markup to be less.

- Remember that there are two ways to figure a markup rate–on cost and on selling price. When a retailer quotes a markup rate, it is usually the rate based on the selling price.

SECTION 2 EXERCISES

In Exercises 1–12, find the missing quantities.

Merchandise	Cost (C)	Selling Price (S)	Markup (M)	Markup Rate on Cost (R)	Markup Rate on Selling Price (r)
1. Watch	$26.97	$49.95	_____	_____	_____
2. Bicycle	$71.97	$119.95	_____	_____	_____
3. Sleeping bag	$89.97	_____	$61.98	_____	_____
4. Calculator	$42.97	_____	$12.89	_____	_____
5. Automobile	_____	$19,869.00	$1,787.00	_____	_____
6. Lawn Mower	_____	$269.00	$52.26	_____	_____
7. Diamond Ring	_____	$4,250.00	_____	_____	31.8%
8. Stereo System	_____	$429.95	_____	_____	33.5%
9. Battery Charger	_____	$54.39	_____	81.5%	_____
10. Gas Lantern	_____	$69.95	_____	55.5%	_____
11. Camera	$107.97	_____	_____	85.2%	_____
12. Freezer	$480.00	_____	_____	$33\frac{1}{3}\%$	_____

13. A furniture store sells a kitchen table that cost $366.00 at a markup rate of 45% on the selling price. What is the selling price of the table? What is the markup rate on cost?

Selling Price: _____

Markup Rate On Cost: _____

14. A sporting goods store sells a tent which cost the store $212.50 at a markup rate of 25% on selling price. What is the selling price of the tent? What is the markup rate on cost?

Selling Price: _____

Markup Rate On Cost: _____

15. Amy Dobson sells cosmetics on a part-time basis through a home distributorship. If Amy's retail sales average $500.00 per week with an average markup rate on selling price of 30%, how much would Amy make in a year?

Answer: _____

16. Greg Tomsic is planning to buy a racing bicycle which has a cost to the dealer of $522.00. Greg's uncle works for a cycle dealership that sells this type of bike and tells Greg that he can buy the bike through him at a markup rate of only 10%. Greg interpreted his uncle's statement to mean that Greg could get the bike for $52.20 + $522.00 = $574.20. (In other words, Greg thought the 10% markup rate was based on cost.) If Greg's uncle actually based the 10% markup on selling price, how much did Greg have to pay for the bike?

Answer: _____

17. A small computer desk cost a retailer $185.00 and the accompanying chair cost $43.00. In a special sale, the retailer offers the chair "free" to customers who purchase the desk. Find the selling price of the desk if the retailer prices it so that he will still have the equivalent of a 12% markup rate based on the cost of *both* items.

Answer: _____

18. A riding lawn mower and grass catcher cost a retailer $875.00 and $69.00 respectively. During a special sale, the grass catcher was given "free" with the purchase of the mower. Find the selling price of the mower if the retailer prices it so that he will still have the equivalent of a 15% markup rate based on the cost of *both* items.

Answer: _____

19. A store has a special sale in which a few loss leader items are sold at cost in order to attract customers. During one day of the sale, the store sold $1,864.00 at cost and $14,587.00 at the regular selling price. Find the cost of all items sold if the total sale that day had an average markup rate on cost of 20%.

Answer: _____

20. Jill Carlton manages the produce department at a supermarket. The cost of a 100-pound box of bananas is $28.60. From past experience, Jill estimates that 10% of the bananas will spoil before they are sold. At what price per pound should Jill sell bananas to give the supermarket an average markup rate on cost of 30%?

Answer: _____

21. Tony Frasier works at a men's clothing store. The store's cost for a shipment of 12 dozen T-shirts is $1,044.00. If Tony sells 65 of the shirts for $15.00 each, then reduces the selling price to $11.95 and sells 60 more, and finally sells the remaining 19 T-shirts at a close-out sale price of $7.95 each, what is the store's average markup rate on cost for these shirts?

Answer: _____

Section 3
Discounts

In Section 2, we discussed the fact that the selling price of an item depends upon *where* you buy the item. Full-service department stores, specialty shops, and small convenience stores usually have higher prices than minimal service discount stores, catalog services, and factory outlet stores. Of course, an experienced shopper knows that under some circumstances, a full-service department store may actually have lower prices than a so-called discount store. The only hard and fast rule for determining where you can get the best price is to shop around and compare.

There are many circumstances under which a retailer is willing to lower the regular selling price. This may be done with the ever popular store-wide sale, or by giving discounts to customers who pay cash or buy in quantity, or even on a one-to-one basis through old-fashioned price haggling. Whatever the setting, the result may mean a lower price for the consumer.

We call a retailer's regular price for an item the **list price** and the reduced price the **sale price** (or discount price). The difference in these two prices is called the **discount** (or markdown). That is,

Discount = List Price − Sale Price,

$$D = L - S.$$

Note that, as in Section 2, S represents the actual price the customer pays. As in the case of markup, the most common way to list a discount is as a rate or percentage based upon the list price. That is,

$$\text{Discount Rate} = \frac{\text{Discount}}{\text{List Price}},$$

$$r = \frac{D}{L}. \qquad \blacklozenge$$

EXAMPLE 1 Finding the discount and the discount rate

During a "mid-summer sale," a lawn mower listed at $299.95 is on sale for $209.99. Find the discount and the discount rate.

SOLUTION

The discount is

$$D = L - S = \$299.95 - \$209.99 = \$89.96.$$

The discount rate is

$$r = \frac{D}{L} = \frac{\$89.96}{\$299.95} \approx 0.2999 \approx 30.0\%. \qquad \blacklozenge$$

Try One!

During a "Fourth of July Sale," a furniture store advertises that its most popular couch which regularly sells for $799.95 is now on sale for $679.96. What is the discount D and the discount rate r?

Discount = _____

Discount Rate = _____

Discount stores and catalog showrooms usually quote list prices along with their "discounted" prices in order to emphasize the supposed savings customers are receiving. Frequently, the quoted list prices are unrealistically high and do not accurately represent the going price of an item. The prices used in the next example are a case in point and represent prices from a catalog showroom and a full-service department store.   ◆

EXAMPLE 2   Comparing discount rates

A catalog showroom's prices on a blender and color television were compared with a department store's prices on the same two items.

Item	List Price	Catalog Showroom Price	Department Store Price
Blender	$51.00	$33.97	$39.93
Color TV	$249.95	$221.97	$221.95

What is the implied catalog discount rate on each item? What is the actual discount rate, assuming the list price to be the department store's price?

SOLUTION

Blender: The implied discount (using $L = \$51.00$) is

$$D = L - S = \$51.00 - \$33.97 = \$17.03$$

and the implied discount rate is

$$r = \frac{D}{L} = \frac{\$17.03}{\$51.00} \approx 0.3339 \approx 33.4\%.$$

The actual discount (using $L = \$39.93$) is

$$D = L - S = \$39.93 - \$33.97 = \$5.96$$

and the actual discount rate is

$$r = \frac{D}{L} = \frac{\$5.96}{\$39.93} \approx 0.1493 \approx 14.9\%.$$

Color TV: The implied discount on the television (using L = \$249.95) is

$$D = L - S = \$249.95 - \$221.97 = \$27.98$$

and the implied discount rate is

$$r = \frac{D}{L} = \frac{\$27.98}{\$249.95} \approx 0.1119 \approx 11.2\%.$$

In reality, this is not a discount at all since the television set could be purchased for 2¢ less at the department store. ◆

Try one!

If a catalog showroom quotes the price of a gold ring to be \$125.00 and claims the list price is \$162.50, what is the implied discount rate? What is the actual discount rate assuming that the local department store sells the same ring for \$130.00?

Implied Discount Rate: _____

Actual Discount Rate: _____

In Examples 1 and 2, we used the two basic formulas for discount and discount rate. From these basic formulas, we can derive the following useful forms:

Sale Price = List Price − Discount

$$S = L - D$$

List Price = Sale Price + Discount

$$L = S + D$$

Discount = (Discount Rate)(List Price)

$$D = rL$$

$$\text{List Price} = \frac{\text{Sale Price}}{1 - \text{Discount Rate}}$$

$$L = \frac{S}{1 - r} \qquad \blacklozenge$$

EXAMPLE 3   Finding the sale price given the list price and discount rate

A variety store advertises 40% off on all summer tanning products. If a bottle of suntan oil lists for $4.89, what is the sale price?

SOLUTION

Since the discount rate is 40%, we have $r = 0.40$. The discount is

$$D = rL = (0.40)(\$4.89) \approx \$1.96.$$

Therefore, the sale price of the suntan oil is

$$S = L - D = \$4.89 - \$1.96 = \$2.93. \qquad \blacklozenge$$

Try one!

A music store advertises 15% off on all compact discs. If a particular compact disc lists for $14.98, what is its sale price?

Answer: _____

EXAMPLE 4 **Finding the list price given the sale price and discount rate**

A golf jacket is marked down 33% from its list price. If the sale price is $33.47, what is the list price? What is the discount?

SOLUTION

Since $S = \$33.47$ and $r = 33\% = 0.33$, the list price is

$$L = \frac{S}{1 - r} = \frac{\$33.47}{1 - 0.33} \approx \$49.96$$

and the discount is

$$D = L - S = \$49.96 - \$33.47 = \$16.49.$$

◆

Try one!

A winter coat is marked down 25% from its list price. If the sale price is $119.96, what is the list price?

Answer: _____

| EXAMPLE 5 | **Finding the discount given the list price and discount rate** |

Alice and Mark Calder are planning a vacation. The regular round trip airfare is $484.00. If Alice and Mark are willing to pay for their tickets one month in advance, the airline will give them a 20% discount. How much will they save with the discount plan?

SOLUTION

Since $L = \$484.00$ and $r = 20\% = 0.20$, the discount is

$$D = rL = (0.20)(\$484.00) = \$96.80.$$

Therefore, Alice and Mark could save $96.80 by paying for the tickets in advance. ◆

Try one!

John Grant is planning a business trip. He has to leave on a Wednesday and will be staying through to the following Tuesday. The regular round trip airfare is $650.00; however, the ticket agent tells John that since he is staying over a Saturday night, he qualifies for the supersaver fare which is a 45% discount off of the regular fare. How much will he save with the supersaver fare?

Answer: _____

EXAMPLE 6   **Finding the discount given the list price and discount rate**

Jean Philips needs ten bottles of sparkling water for a party. As her purchase is being boxed up, the sales clerk tells Jean that she can get a 10% discount if she buys a case of twelve. If the sparkling water costs $1.49 per bottle, how much *more* would Jean have to pay for the two additional bottles?

SOLUTION

If Jean buys ten bottles, the total price would be

   Total Price $= 10(\$1.49) = \$14.90.$

If Jean buys 12 bottles, the list price would be

   $L = 12(\$1.49) = \$17.88,$

and the discount would be

   $D = rL = (0.10)(\$17.88) \approx \$1.79.$

Thus, the sale price for the 12 bottles would be

$$S = L - D = \$17.88 - \$1.79 = \$16.09.$$

Therefore, Jean would only have to pay a total of

$$\$16.09 - \$14.90 = \$1.19$$

for the two extra bottles. ◆

Try one!

While planning their vacation, the Calders made reservations at a resort hotel. The charge per night at this hotel was $89.50 and the Calders wanted to reserve a room for six nights. They found out from the reservation clerk that if they stay a seventh night, the total bill would be discounted 10%. If the Calders decide to stay the extra night, how much *more* would they actually pay for the seventh night in the hotel?

Answer: _____

Before concluding this section, it is worth pointing out that while there are many genuine bargains available, a conscientious shopper should take heed of the old adage "Let the buyer beware." The marketplace abounds in deceptive retailing practices designed to mislead consumers. Here are a few of the common ones.

Inflated List Prices

Many retailers quote list prices or "manufacturer's suggested retail prices" that are not truly representative of market value. This practice leads consumers to believe that they are obtaining substantial discounts when in fact the discounts may be minimal or even nonexistent.

Bait and Switch

This practice involves advertising an item at a very low price. When a customer shows up to purchase the item (the bait), the salesperson tries to discourage the purchase of the sale item and attempts to sell a higher priced product (the switch).

Hidden Costs

Buying services and catalog services often have membership fees, service charges, and postage fees which reduce or eliminate the discounts they claim to offer.

Special Sale Merchandise

When a store offers a sale, customers usually assume that the store is lowering its price on regularly stocked items of high quality. Unfortunately, it is not uncommon for a store to order lower quality merchandise just for the special sale, thus misleading the customer who believes he or she is getting a bargain on regularly stocked high quality goods. ◆

Important Terms

D, Discount (or mark down)

L, List Price

r, Discount Rate

S, Sale Price

Important Formulas

$$D = L - S$$
$$S = L - D$$
$$L = S + D$$
$$r = \frac{D}{L}$$
$$D = rL$$
$$L = \frac{S}{1 - r}$$

CONSUMER HINTS

- Before making a major purchase, check the prices at different types of retailers such as a department store, a catalog service, and a discount store.

- Be on the lookout for sales. Some of the best sales occur when retailers are trying to get rid of seasonal items or "last year's models."

- Ask about the discount policies. You may be able to obtain a discount if you buy in quantity, pay cash, are buying for business or charity, are over 65, or any number of other reasons.

- Don't be misled by "trumped up" discounts. Remember that the important figure is the amount you are asked to pay.

- Keep in mind that the greatest "savings" on a bargain item may be not to purchase it at all.

A Calendar of What's on Sale and When*

JANUARY

Christmas items

White goods

Shoes, clothing

Fabrics

Toys

FEBRUARY

President's Day Sales

Cars

Furniture, floor coverings

Mattresses

Major appliances

MARCH

Housewares

China, glassware

Air conditioners

APRIL

After-Easter sales

Women's dresses, coats

Men's and boys' clothing

Soaps, cleaning supplies

MAY

Memorial Day sales

Television sets

White goods

JUNE

Rug cleaning

Storm windows

JULY

Summer clearance sales

Shoes, clothing, swimsuits

White goods

Jewelry

Furniture

Refrigerators, washing machines

Garden supplies

Floor coverings

AUGUST

Back-to-school specials

Cars, tires

Furniture

Summer clothing

White goods

Coats, furs

Garden equipment

Painting supplies

Camping equipment

Cameras

SEPTEMBER

Labor Day specials

Back-to-school specials

Cars (end of model year)

Tires

Clothing

Housewares

China, glassware

OCTOBER

Columbus Day, fall sales

Cars (last of old models)

Coats

Lingerie

Infant needs

NOVEMBER

Furs

Election Day sales

Veterans Day sales

Thanksgiving weekend sales

DECEMBER

Men's, boys' suits, coats

Christmas sales:

    gift items,

    decorations,

    winter merchandise

* From time to time, when stores become overstocked in a particular category of merchandise, they will run item sales that may not appear on this calendar.

-National Retail Federation (NRF)

SECTION 3   EXERCISES

In Exercises 1–14, find the missing quantities.

Merchandise	List Price (L)	Sale Price (S)	Discount (D)	Discount Rate (r)
1. Wheel alignment	$45.99	$36.79	_____	_____
2. Car battery	$50.99	$45.99	_____	_____
3. Steak dinner	$10.85	$8.75	_____	_____
4. Shock absorber	$34.95	_____	$10.63	_____
5. Recliner chair	$349.99	_____	$55.26	_____
6. T-shirt	$16.99	_____	$7.34	_____
7. Sneakers	$69.97	_____	_____	20%
8. Watch	$119.90	_____	_____	50%
9. CD player	$189.00	_____	_____	30%
10. Gallon of paint	_____	$14.99	_____	21.5%
11. Couch	_____	$849.00	_____	16.5%
12. Summer blouse	_____	$34.95	_____	$33\frac{1}{3}\%$
13. Beach towel	_____	$10.88	$4.99	_____
14. Magazine	_____	$2.51	$0.44	_____

15. A catalog showroom gives the list price of an electric typewriter as $345.00 and their price as $229.97. A mail order catalog has the same typewriter for $297.99 plus a $4.14 shipping charge. Find the discount rate for each outlet based on the catalog showroom's list price.

Showroom Rate: _____

Mail-Order Rate: _____

16. A catalog showroom gives the list price of a small wall safe as $194.00 and their price as $147.87. A mail order catalog has the same safe for $157.95 plus a $24.14 shipping charge. Find the discount rate for each outlet based on the catalog showroom's list price.

Showroom Rate: _____

Mail-Order Rate: _____

17. A mail order catalog has automotive shock absorbers for $48.99 a pair plus a shipping charge of $2.69. A local store has a special sale with 25% off the list price of $63.99. Which is the better bargain?

Answer: _____

18. A department store is offering a discount of 20% on a winter goose down coat with a list price of $239.95. A mail order catalog has the same coat for $188.95 plus $4.32 for shipping. Which is the better bargain?

Answer: _____

19. A women's clothing store is having a clearance sale on spring merchandise. All spring items are reduced by $33\frac{1}{3}\%$ for one week. Furthermore, every item which doesn't sell during the first sale week will be reduced 25% *off the sale price*. A dress with a list price of $48.95 went through both price reductions. What is the sale price after the second reduction and what is the corresponding discount rate based on the original list price?

Sale Price After Second Reduction: _____

Discount Rate (based on list price): _____

20. A suitcase with a list price of $159.95 was discounted three times before it was finally sold. It was first reduced by 40% (on the list price), then by 15% (on the sale price), and then by 10% (on the second sale price).

a. What was the final sale price of the suitcase?

Answer: _____

b. What is the final discount rate based on the original list price?

Answer: _____

Section 4

Utility Bills

Most consumers have little or no choice in determining what utilities to buy or from what company to buy them. There is usually only one local telephone and one electric company serving a given area and energy choices for heating are generally limited to electricity, natural gas, propane, and oil. Furthermore, private water and sewage systems are increasingly more difficult to obtain. Whether purchased from private or public sources, the costs for utilities have caused many consumers to search for ways to economize. There are, in fact, many ways to reduce utility costs without drastically altering one's standard of living.

For some consumers, significant cost reductions can be experienced by simply being less wasteful. In other cases, cost reductions can be achieved by changes in the time of day usage such as with electricity and telephone service.

In this section, we will focus our study on three basic utilities: telephone service, electricity, and home fuels. The rate schedules for these utilities vary from one company to another and in order to make the most economical use of utilities, consumers should become familiar with the rate schedules of their own utilities.

TELEPHONE SERVICE

A typical monthly telephone bill includes up to four basic charges: 1) **local service charges**, 2) **long-distance charges**, 3) surcharges, and 4) taxes. The local service charge depends upon the company and type of services selected (i.e. call waiting, caller identification, and voice mailbox, to mention a few), the number of telephone lines, and in some areas there is a charge for touch-tone service. Surcharges may vary from place to place and by month and can be either a charge or credit to the consumer. Finally, there may be local, state, or federal taxes figured on the total of all charges.

EXAMPLE 1   Determining the cost for local telephone service

The Markle family lives in suburban Erie, PA and has two telephone lines in their home, one for making calls and the other for their computer modem. The monthly charge for each line is $19.60. Additionally, one of the lines has the following extra services: 1) call waiting which costs $2.50 per month, 2) voice mailbox which costs $6.95 per month. Find the Markle's total local monthly charges if there is a 3% federal tax, and a surcharge of 0.2% on local services.

SOLUTION

Since there are two telephone lines and two special features, the calculation of local service charges is

$39.20	two telephone lines = (2)($19.60)
2.50	call waiting
+ 6.95	voice mailbox
$48.65	Total Charges TC

$$\text{Total Bill} = TC + \text{Tax} + \text{Surcharge}$$

$$= (TC) + (TC)(0.03) + (TC)(0.002)$$

$$= \$48.65 + \$1.4595 + \$0.0973$$

$$= \$50.2068$$

$$\approx \$50.21.$$ ◆

Try one!

The Hagerman family lives in northern Florida and has three telephone lines in their home, one for the parents to use, one for the kids, and the other for their fax machine. The monthly charge for each line is $15.80. Additionally, one of the lines has voice mailbox service which costs $6.50 per month. Find the Hagerman's total local monthly charges if there is a 3% federal tax and a surcharge of 0.19% on local services.

Answer: _____

While most consumers have no choice of local telephone company, a wide variety of options is available when choosing a long-distance carrier. Each carrier has a basic direct-dial schedule of rates in addition to a multitude of calling plans that, depending on the consumer's use of long distance, may offer savings on long-distance charges. For example, Table 4 shows the rate schedules for calls originating in Erie, PA for two different companies. Company A's rates differ by time of day and distance of call, as well as in-region and in-state calling. Company B offers a simpler plan that is time, but not distance, dependent.

TABLE 4

Company A   Rates depend on mileage between parties.

Direct dial rates per minute from Erie, PA to:	Weekday*	Evening	Night/Weekend
Atlanta, GA	$0.27	$0.17	$0.14
Boston, MA	$0.27	$0.17	$0.13
Chicago, IL	$0.27	$0.15	$0.13
Detroit, MI	$0.26	$0.15	$0.13
Honolulu, HI	$0.35	$0.23	$0.17
Los Angeles, CA	$0.30	$0.18	$0.16
Within PA, but outside Erie region	$0.29	$0.19	$0.19
Within Erie region			
First Minute:	$0.14	$0.11	$0.09
Additional Minutes:	$0.12	$0.10	$0.06

*Weekday: 8 a.m. - 5 p.m, Evening: 5 p.m. - 11 p.m., Night/Weekend: 11 p.m. - 8 a.m., all day Saturday, and Sunday until 5 p.m.

Company B   Rates are the same to all United States locations.

Direct dial rates per minute from anywhere in the U.S. to:	Weekday**	Night/Weekend
Anywhere in the U.S.	$0.25	$0.10

**Weekday: 7 a.m. - 7 p.m., Night/Weekend: 7 p.m. - 7 a.m. as well as all day Saturday and Sunday.

EXAMPLE 2 **Finding the cost of long distance calls using two different calling plans**

Use Table 4 to determine the cost of a ten-minute call from Erie to Detroit at 2 p.m. on Thursday using Company A, and then Company B.

SOLUTION

Since this is a weekday call, the Company A charge is $0.26 per minute. Therefore, the total cost for this call is:

Total Cost = (10)($0.26) = $2.60.

This same call using Company B has a $0.25 per minute charge. Therefore, the total cost for the call is:

Total Cost = (10)($0.25) = $2.50.   ◆

EXAMPLE 3 **Finding the cost of long distance calls using two different calling plans**

Use Table 4 to determine the cost of a ten-minute call from Erie to Detroit at 2 p.m. on Sunday using Company A, and then Company B.

SOLUTION

Since this is a night/weekend call, the Company A charge is $0.13 per minute. The total cost is:

Total Cost = (10)($0.13) = $1.30.

Company B's per minute charge is $0.10 making the total cost:

Total Cost = (10)($0.10) = $1.00.   ◆

EXAMPLE 4 **Finding the cost of long distance calls using two different calling plans**

Use Table 4 to determine the cost of a ten-minute call from Erie to Detroit at 6 p.m. on Friday using Company A, and then Company B.

SOLUTION

This call is during the evening rate hours for Company A and has a per minute charge of $0.15 making the total cost:

Total Cost = (10)($0.15) = $1.50.

Company B's rate for this same time is $0.25 so the total cost of the call is:

Total Cost = (10)($0.25) = $2.50.   ◆

Try one!

Roger Foster, who lives in Erie, PA, has a daughter in college in Atlanta, GA. He usually calls her on Thursdays in the evening around dinner time since he knows she will be home. They speak for an average of 15 minutes.

a. If Roger makes the calls at 6:00 p.m., which telephone company would cost him less and by how much?

Answer: _____

b. If Roger makes the calls at 7:30 p.m., which telephone company would cost him less and by how much?

Answer: _____

Examples 2–4 demonstrate that both the time of call and choice of calling plan can affect the cost of a long-distance call. Another factor that can influence the price of a long-distance call with some companies is whether the consumer is calling in-state or out-of-state.

EXAMPLE 5   Determining the costs for in-state calls

Kelley Jensen made a direct-dial call from Erie, PA to her mother who lives within the Erie region. Her call was made at 12:00 noon on a Monday and lasted 17 minutes.

    a. Determine the cost of this call using Company A.

    b. Decide if Kelley should consider switching to Company B. This is the time she always makes the calls to her mother and she rarely makes other long-distance calls.

SOLUTION

a. Since this call was made within the Erie region during weekday rates, there is a $0.14 charge for the first minute and a $0.12 charge for each additional minute. Thus, the cost of making this call using Company A would be:

$$\text{Cost} = \$0.14 + (16)(\$0.12)$$

$$= \$0.14 + \$1.92$$

$$= \$2.06.$$

b. Company B's rate for all calls made at this time is $0.25 per minute. Therefore, the cost of making this call using Company B would be:

$$\text{Cost} = (17)(\$0.25)$$

$$= \$4.25.$$

From this information, Kelley can conclude that she should stay with Company A since it provides better rates for her particular pattern of long-distance calling.   ◆

In Example 5, it is important to note that the time of day significantly affected the cost of the call. Had Kelley made the call to her mother at 8 p.m. on Monday, companies A and B would have differed by only $0.01. Remember, too, that when a consumer subscribes to a long-distance provider, all direct-dial calls made from the home and billed through the local telephone company must be made using that provider. One cannot normally make some calls using Company A and other calls using Company B. Therefore, careful consideration of various plans, as well as individual calling patterns, is a good idea when selecting a long-distance carrier.

ELECTRIC AND HOME FUEL SERVICE

Most utility companies follow one or more of four basic types of rate schedules. The first is called the **declining-block rate schedule** where the cost per unit drops as consumption increases. Such a rate rewards heavy users with lower unit costs. Due to conservation, there has been a trend away from this type of rate schedule over the past decade. The second is the **inverted-block** rate schedule in which the cost per unit increases as consumption increases. The third and most common type of schedule is called the **flat rate schedule** in which the cost per unit is the same no matter how many units are used. Still a fourth alternative is the **time-of-use schedule** (similar to that used for long-distance calls) in which the cost per unit is highest on weekdays when the demand is high and lowest at night and on weekends when the demand is low.

A typical monthly utility bill includes up to five basic charges: 1) the **base rate *BR*** on the number of units used, 2) a **surcharge *S*** on the base rate, 3) a **basic monthly service charge *MSC,*** 4) a **fuel-cost adjustment *FCA*** which can be a charge or credit and varies from month to month, and 5) taxes. The units for measuring consumption of utilities are cubic feet for natural gas, gallons for fuel oil, pounds or gallons for propane, tons for coal, and kilowatt-hours for electricity. A **kilowatt-hour** (kwh) is the amount of electricity used by a 100-watt bulb burning for ten hours. That is,

$$(100 \text{ watts})(10 \text{ hours}) = 1000 \text{ watt-hours} = 1 \text{ kilowatt-hour}.$$

EXAMPLE 6   Finding the number of kilowatt-hours

Bill and Joyce Ostrum are in the habit of leaving their kitchen light on 24 hours a day. If this light has two 75-watt bulbs, how many kilowatt-hours does the light use in a month? If the Ostrum's utility company charges 6¢ per kilowatt-hour, what does it cost to keep this light burning? (Assume the month has 30 days.)

SOLUTION

We begin by finding the number of watt-hours used by this light in a month:

$$\text{Watt-hours} = (\# \text{ bulbs})(\# \text{ watts/bulb})(\# \text{ hours/day})(\# \text{ days})$$

$$= (2)(75)(24)(30)$$

$$= 108,000 \text{ watt-hours}$$

Since 1000 watt-hours equals 1 kilowatt-hour, we divide this figure by 1000 to obtain the number of kilowatt-hours:

$$\frac{108,000 \text{ watt-hours}}{1000 \text{ watt-hours per kilowatt-hour}} = 108 \text{ kilowatt-hours.}$$

At 6¢ per kilowatt-hour, the monthly cost of burning this light is:

$$\text{Monthly Cost} = (\$0.06)(108) = \$6.48. \qquad \blacklozenge$$

Try one!

Bill and Joyce Ostrum (from Example 6) decide to conserve energy and put a 35-watt nightlight in the kitchen that will stay on 24 hours a day rather than keeping on the kitchen light that has two 75-watt bulbs. Remember, their electric company charges 6¢ per kwh.

a. What does it cost to keep this new nightlight burning for a month?

Answer: _____

b. How much do the Ostrum's save on their electric bill?

Answer: _____

EXAMPLE 7 Finding a monthly bill using a declining-block rate schedule

Ann and Philip Garmon buy electricity from a company that uses the following declining-block rate schedule:

I. Base Rates		
	0 to 600 kwh	$0.04906 per kwh
	over 600 kwh	$0.03754 per kwh
II. Basic Monthly Service Charge		$11.00 per month
III. Fuel-Cost Adjustment (Credit)		–$0.00391 per kwh

If the Garmons used 1150 kilowatt-hours in June, what is their total bill? (Assume there is no tax on electricity in this state.)

SOLUTION

To calculate the charges based on a declining-block rate schedule, we must first find the number of units in each block. The declining-block rate schedule used by the Garmons' electric company breaks down as follows:

Block	Number of Units in Block	Rate
0 to 600 kwh	600 kwh	$0.04906
over 600 kwh	550 kwh	$0.03754

Thus, the base rate BR for the 1150 kilowatt-hours used by the Garmons is

$$BR = (600)(\$0.04906) + (550)(\$0.03754)$$

$$= \$29.436 + \$20.647$$

$$= \$50.083$$

$$\approx \$50.08.$$

The basic monthly service charge *MSC* is $11.00.

Finally, the fuel-cost adjustment *FCA* is

$$FCA = (1150)(\$0.00391)$$

$$= \$4.4965$$

$$\approx \$4.50 \text{ (credit)}.$$

To determine the Garmons' total electric bill for June we must add together the base rate and the basic monthly service charge and then, since it is a credit, subtract the fuel-cost adjustment:

$$\text{Total Bill} = BR + MSC - FCA$$

$$= \$50.08 + \$11.00 - \$4.50$$

$$= \$56.58. \qquad \blacklozenge$$

Try one!

Use the declining-block rate schedule in Example 7 to determine the Garmons' total electric bill if they use 935 kwh.

Answer: _____

EXAMPLE 8   Finding a monthly bill using a flat rate schedule

Roberta Clark owns a 20-year-old, seven-room, two-story house. She purchases natural gas from a company that has the following flat rate schedule:

Basic Monthly Service Charge	$11.35
Base Rate per cubic foot of gas	$0.0058354
Surcharge per cubic foot of gas	$0.0001351
State Tax of 5% on all charges	

If Roberta used 21,000 cubic feet of gas in December, what is her total bill for that month?

SOLUTION

The base rate BR is

$$BR = (21{,}000)(\$0.0058354) \approx \$122.54.$$

The surcharge S is

$$S = (21{,}000)(\$0.0001351) \approx \$2.84.$$

The basic monthly service charge MSC is \$11.35.

In order to calculate the state tax, we must first add the monthly charges and then multiply that total by 5%.

$$\text{Tax} = (BR + S + MSC)(5\%)$$

$$= (\$122.54 + \$2.84 + \$11.35)(0.05)$$

$$\approx \$6.84.$$

Therefore, Roberta's total gas bill for the month of December is

$$\text{Total Bill} = BR + S + MSC + \text{Tax}$$

$$= \$122.54 + \$2.84 + \$11.35 + \$6.84$$

$$= \$143.57. \qquad\blacklozenge$$

Try one!

Suppose Roberta Clark used 8000 cubic feet of gas in August. Using the flat rate schedule in Example 8, find Roberta's total monthly gas bill for August.

Answer: _____

EXAMPLE 9   Finding a monthly bill using an inverted-block rate schedule

Roberta Clark purchases electricity from a utility company that has the following inverted-block rate schedule:

   I. Base Rates

        0 to 700 kwh $0.0675 per kwh

        over 700 kwh $0.0785 per kwh

  II. Surcharge on the Base Rate   3%

 III. Basic Monthly Service Charge $7.50 per month

 IV. Fuel-Cost Adjustment (Charge) $0.0125 per kwh

If Roberta used 980 kwh during the month of April, what was her total electric bill?

SOLUTION

We must first find the number of kwh in each block.

Block	Number of Units in Block	Rate
0 to 700 kwh	700 kwh	$0.0675
over 700 kwh	280 kwh	$0.0785

Thus, the base rate BR for the 980 kwh used by Roberta is

$$BR = (700)(\$0.0675) + (280)(\$0.0785)$$

$$= \$69.23.$$

The surcharge S on the base rate is

$$S = (3\%)(BR)$$

$$= (0.03)(\$69.23)$$

$$\approx \$2.08.$$

The basic monthly service charge MSC is $7.50.

The fuel-cost adjustment FCA is

$$\text{Fuel-Cost Adjustment} = (980)(\$0.0125) \approx \$12.25.$$

To determine Roberta's total electric bill for April, we must add together the base rate, the surcharge, the basic monthly service charge, and the fuel-cost adjustment. Note that in this example, the fuel-cost adjustment is a charge instead of a credit.

$$\text{Total Bill} = BR + S + MSC + FCA$$

$$= \$69.23 + \$2.08 + \$7.50 + \$12.25$$

$$= \$91.06.$$ ◆

Try one!

Using the inverted-block rate schedule in Example 9, find the total monthly electric bill if Roberta used 1050 kwh in the month of July.

Answer: _____

EXAMPLE 10 Combination of the declining-block and inverted-block rate schedules

A particular electric company has the following rate schedule:

I. Base Rates

   A. June through September

      1. 0 to 800 kwh $0.06753 per kwh

      2. over 800 kwh $0.07828 per kwh

   B. October through May

      1. 0 to 800 kwh $0.06753 per kwh

      2. over 800 kwh $0.04782 per kwh

II. Basic Monthly Service Charge $7.50 per month

III. Fuel-Cost Adjustment (Charge) $0.01229 per kwh

If Edna and Scott Parker used 975 kwh during the month of September, what was their total bill?

SOLUTION

Since the month in question is September, we will use the base rate schedule in part A. Notice that this section of the base rate schedule is an inverted block since the cost per unit increases as consumption increases. To find the base rate we first need to determine the number of units in each block:

Block	Number of Units in Block	Rate
0 to 800 kwh	800 kwh	$0.06753
over 800 kwh	175 kwh	$0.07828

Thus, the base rate BR for the 975 kilowatt-hours used is

$$BR = (800)(\$0.06753) + (175)(\$0.07828)$$

$$= \$67.723$$

$$\approx \$67.72.$$

The basic monthly service charge MSC is $7.50.

The fuel-cost adjustment FCA is

$$FCA = (975)(\$0.01229) = \$11.98275 \approx \$11.98.$$

To determine the Parkers' total monthly bill, we add together the base rate, the basic monthly service charge and the fuel-cost adjustment:

$$\text{Total Bill} = BR + MSC + FCA$$

$$= \$67.72 + \$7.50 + \$11.98$$

$$= \$87.20. \qquad \blacklozenge$$

Try one!

Using the rate schedule in Example 10, determine the Parkers' total monthly bill if they used 975 kwh in October, the same number of kilowatt-hours they used in September.

Answer: _____

EXAMPLE 11 **Comparing utility bills**

Roberta Clark (see Example 8) decides to reduce her utility bills by installing storm windows and putting additional insulation in the ceiling areas of her home. The storm windows are predicted to reduce fuel consumption by 20% and the insulation by 15%. In addition, Roberta has decided to set her thermostat at 68°F in the day and 60°F at night. She expects these lower temperatures to cut consumption by 5%.

a. If Roberta used 21,000 cubic feet during December without these improvements, how much should she expect to use next December with the improvements?

b. Assuming the rates remain the same as in Example 8, what should Roberta expect her bill to be next December?

SOLUTION

a. The cumulative effect of Roberta's conservation efforts will total

20% + 15% + 5% = 40%.

Since she used 21,000 cubic feet of gas this December, she can expect her usage to drop to

Next December's Usage = $21,000 - (0.40)(21,000)$

$$= 21,000 - 8,400$$

$$= 12,600 \text{ cubic feet.}$$

b. Recall that the flat rate schedule from Example 8 is as follows:

Basic Monthly Service Charge	$11.35
Base Rate per cubic foot of gas	$0.0058354
Surcharge per cubic foot of gas	$0.0001351
State Tax of 5% on all charges	

Roberta can expect next December's bill to be

Total Bill = $BR + S + MSC + \text{Tax}$

$$= (12,600)(\$0.0058354) + (12,600)(\$0.0001351)$$
$$+ \$11.35 + \text{Tax}$$

$$\approx \$75.53 + \$1.70 + \$11.35$$
$$+ (\$73.53 + \$1.70 + \$11.35)(0.05)$$

$$\approx \$86.58 + \$4.33$$

$$= \$90.91. \qquad \blacklozenge$$

There are many ways that the average consumer can reduce monthly utility bills. The following "energy efficiency" quiz was prepared by the Federal Energy Administration. A score of 90 or above shows your house to be in good energy shape. A score between 75 and 90 reveals definite areas for improvement. A score below 75 indicates you are wasting a substantial amount of money.

Energy Efficiency Quiz

INSULATION:

Score 30 points for 7 inches or more, 25 points for 5 or 6 inches, and 20 points for 3 or 4 inches.

_____

If there is unheated space beneath your house, add 5 points for an insulated floor. Score 5 points for no space.

_____

THERMOSTAT:

If you set the thermostat at 68°F or less during the day in winter, score 5 points, 4 for 69°F, 3 for 70°F, 2 for 71°F, and 1 for 72°F.

_____

In winter, if you set the thermostat at 60°F or less overnight, score 10 points, 9 points for 61°F, 8 for 62°F, and so forth.

_____

If you set the air-conditioning at 80°F, score 5 points, 4 for 79°F, 3 for 78°F, 2 for 77°F, and 1 for 76°F. Score 5 points for no air-conditioning.

_____

AIR LEAKAGE:

If no air leaks in around window, score 10 points. If no air enters around doors, score an additional 2 points.

_____

If you keep the fireplace damper closed or block air flow when not in use, score 3 points. Score 3 points if you don't have a fireplace.

_____

If the outside temperature often falls below 30°F and you have storm window, score 16 points. If the temperature rarely or never falls below 30°F, score 16 points.

_____

If temperatures frequently drop below 30°F and you have storm doors, or if temperatures rarely drop below 30°F, score 1 point.

_____

MISCELLANEOUS:

If you close the curtains and shades to sunlight in summer and open them during the day in winter, score 5 points.

_____

If the water heater is adjusted to 120°F, score 5 points. For 140°F, score 2 points.

_____

If you run the dishwasher, clothes washer and dryer only with full loads, score 1 point.

_____

If you open the dishwasher to let the dishes air-dry, score 1 point. If you have no dishwasher, score 1 point.

_____

If the hot water faucets don't drip, score 1 point.

_____

TOTAL:　_____

Important Terms

Base Rate	Declining-Block Rate Schedule
Surcharge	Flat Rate Schedule
Fuel-Cost Adjustment	Inverted-Block Rate Schedule
Local Service Charge	Time-of-Use Rate Schedule
Long Distance Charge	Kilowatt-Hour
Basic Monthly Service Charge	

CONSUMER HINTS

• Remember that long-distance rates are substantially less for calls placed in the evening, at night, or on weekends.

• When choosing a long distance provider, examine the times and places you call as well as the various calling plans available.

• There are three basic ways to reduce utility bills.

   1. The *source of energy* makes a difference. In some parts of the country, electricity is cheaper than natural gas. If you have both gas and electric service in your home, you should choose your appliances (stoves, water heaters clothes dryers, etc.) in such a way as to take advantage of these differences in cost. In some more rural areas of the country, wood, coal or oil may be practical alternatives for heating.

   2. *Insulation* makes a difference. Keeping the outside air out and the inside air in can make substantial differences in both heating and cooling costs.

   3. *Conservation* makes a difference. Your utility bills will be smaller if you are willing to keep your house cooler in the winter, keep it warmer in the summer, use less lighting, and use appliances less.

SECTION 4   EXERCISES

In Exercises 1–10, use the long distance rates from Table 4 on page 70.

1. Using Company A's rates, determine the cost of an 8-minute call from Erie to Chicago at 7:00 p.m. on Saturday.

Answer: _____

2. Using Company A's rates, determine the cost of an 8-minute call from Erie to Chicago at 7:00 p.m. on Wednesday.

Answer: _____

3. Using Company A's rates, determine the cost of an 8-minute call from Erie to within the Erie region at 7:00 p.m. on Saturday.

Answer: _____

4. Using Company A's rates, determine the cost of an 8-minute call from Erie to within the Erie region at 7:00 p.m. on Wednesday.

Answer: _____

5. Using Company B's rates, determine the cost of a 15-minute call from Erie to Boston at 9 a.m. on Tuesday.

Answer: _____

6. Using Company B's rates, determine the cost of a 20-minute call from Erie to Boston at 7:30 p.m. on Tuesday.

Answer: _____

7. Using Company B's rates, determine the cost of a 20-minute call from Erie to Boston at 9:00 a.m. on Tuesday.

Answer: _____

8. In Exercises 6 and 7, how much is saved by calling at night?

Answer: _____

9. Bill Calkins, residing in Erie, calls his parents in Los Angeles every week and they talk an average of 12 minutes each time. Using Company A's rates, determine the yearly savings if Bill made his calls when the night and weekend rates were in effect rather than the weekday rates.

Answer: _____

10. Repeat Exercise 9 using the rates for Company B.

Answer: _____

11. If Bill Calkins (from Exercise 9) decides to make all his calls at 6:00 p.m., which company would cost him less per year and by how much?

Answer: _____

12. Which company costs less if Bill Calkins decides to make his calls at 7:30 p.m.?

Answer: _____

13. The Wang family pays a local service charge of $18.21 per month for their telephone. Their local service options consist of touch-tone service at $1.50 per month, caller identification at $7.00 per month and call waiting at $2.50 per month. Find the total amount due for local services if their bill includes a tax of 3%.

Answer: _____

14. Company A has a special plan that will give a 25% discount off an entire long distance bill if it exceeds $10.00 per month. The Clarks, who live in Erie, called Honolulu for 32 minutes on Monday at 12:00 noon and Boston for 45 minutes on Wednesday at 11:30 p.m. Applying the plan discount, find the discount amount and the long distance charges after the discount for these calls.

Discount: _____

Total Charges: _____

15. Calculate the charges for the two calls in Exercise 14 using Company B's rates (no discounts). Which plan is less expensive (Company B without discounts or Company A with the discount) and by how much?

Answer: _____

16. Janice Morgan has a 150-watt outside security light that is on an average of eight hours per night. If Janice's utility company charges 6.5¢ per kilowatt-hour, what does it cost her to operate the light for one year?

Answer: _____

17. Susan and Don Rice have their electric water heater set at 140°F and at this setting their heater uses about 220 kilowatt-hours of electricity a month. At a setting of 115°F, this heater would use approximately 25% less electricity. How much would Susan and Don save in a year by lowering the setting to 115°F if their electricity costs 4¢ per kwh?

Answer: _____

18. Repeat Exercise 17 if the electricity costs 5.5¢ kwh.

Answer: _____

19. Repeat Exercise 17 if the electricity costs 6.9¢ per kwh.

Answer: _____

20. Use the declining-block rate schedule of Example 7 (page 76) to find the monthly electric bill for 530 kilowatt-hours.

Answer: _____

21. Use the declining block rate schedule of Example 7 (page 76) to find the monthly electric bill for 1130 kilowatt hours.

Answer: _____

22. Nancy Freeman's utility company uses a flat rate schedule of 6.9¢ per kilowatt-hour plus a 5.31% state tax. If Nancy used 980 kilowatt-hours of electricity during a month in which the energy fuel-cost adjustment was a credit of $0.003115 per kilowatt-hour, how much was her electric bill that month?

Answer: _____

23. Using the inverted-block rate schedule of Example 9, find the monthly electric bill for a month in which 945 kwh of electricity is used.

Answer: _____

24. Lou and Florence Harper's gas heating bill during February was $81.67. By purchasing a wood-burning stove, the Harpers were able to reduce their gas bill by 30% the following February. However, during February they burned one-half cord of firewood which they purchased for $50.00 a cord. Did they save any money in February?

Answer: _____

25. Doris and Randy Blakely live in a utility district which provides inexpensive hydro-electricity at a flat rate of $0.008 per kilowatt-hour. During a particular month, their all-electric home used 2840 kilowatt-hours of electricity. Assuming Doris and Randy's electric company has no energy fuel-cost adjustment charge and the state tax is 4.8%, how much was their electric bill that month?

Answer: _____

26. The Johnson family used 845 gallons of fuel oil to heat their house in one year. Find their yearly heating bill if the price of fuel is 79.9¢ per gallon.

Answer: _____

27. A storm window salesman tells the Johnsons that they can reduce their fuel oil consumption by 20% by installing storm windows. If this is true, by how much would the Johnsons reduce their fuel oil bill by installing storm windows?

Answer: _____

28. How many years would it take the Johnsons (from Exercise 27) to pay for the storm windows with their fuel savings if the windows cost $425.00?

Answer: _____

29. a. Using the rate schedule in Example 10, find the amount of the Parker's electric bill if they used 1175 kwh during the month of February.

Answer: _____

b. The Parkers used 1175 kwh of electricity in July as well as in February (see part **a**). Is there a difference in the bills for the two months? If so, which month has the greater bill and by how much?

Answer: _____

Section 5
Spotlight On The Pharmacist

Most pharmacists are responsible for the proper dispensation of medications and the careful maintenance of records. These records are most often computerized so that the pharmacist can easily detect the possibility of any potentially dangerous drug interactions for the patients. There are several different types of places where you can find a pharmacist, including hospitals and clinics, home health care, and the most visible of all places, a community pharmacy.

In the hospital or clinic setting, pharmacists are responsible for advising doctors and nurses on the effects that certain drugs may have on a patient. Additionally, the pharmacist may help doctors with their selection of a particular drug in a patient's course of treatment. The pharmacist will then help the doctor monitor a patient's medication dosage and use upon discharge. Hospital and clinic pharmacists may also be called upon to mix sterile solutions or special compounds.

Home health care pharmacists are responsible for the careful preparation of medications for a patient's use in the home. These pharmacists also closely monitor the patient's course of drug therapy, as well as provide counseling to patients about their medication.

Most people are familiar with community pharmacists. These pharmacists dispense prescriptions, answer customers' questions about over-the-counter drugs, and educate the customers about potential drug interactions if they are taking more than one course of drug therapy. Community pharmacists may also help the customer in the selection of necessary home health care supplies and equipment. Community pharmacists can work in any one of several types of environments, including chain drug stores, independent drug stores, discount stores, and supermarkets.

Full-time, salaried pharmacists can earn up to $60,000 or more per year, depending on their specialty and location. Pharmacists that work in the West tend to make more than those in other areas of the country, and nonindependent retail stores often provide the best benefits, such as health insurance and retirement plans.

Among those pharmacists that work in retail, those who own the pharmacy themselves often earn more per year than salaried pharmacists. Ownership of a pharmacy not only involves the skills already discussed, but also requires the pharmacist to have knowledge of marketing, advertising, and management, since most community pharmacies sell a great deal of nonhealth-related goods and employ members of the community.

Pharmacists in any of these areas will spend most of their time on their feet. They work in very clean and well-lighted areas, and since most pharmacies in both the hospital and the retail industry are open late, and often around the clock, the pharmacist may work evenings, nights, weekends, and even holidays. Pharmacists who own their own stores sometimes work more than fifty hours per week.

The educational requirements involve at least five years of study beyond high school. Entry requirements into most programs include mathematics, chemistry, biology, and physics, as well as social sciences and humanities. Some colleges also require the Pharmacy College Admissions Test (P-CAT). If employment in a retail or community pharmacy is the goal, then, the bachelor's degree in pharmacy is generally acceptable; however, to work in a hospital pharmacy it is becoming necessary to obtain an advanced degree in pharmacy called a Pharm.D. degree. One particular university in the state of Michigan lists the following requirements for registration as a pharmacist: 1) graduation from an accredited college of pharmacy, 2) age of twenty-one, 3) good moral character, 4) completion of a Board–approved internship, and 5) passage of the National Association of Boards of Pharmacy Licensure Examination (NABPLEX), as well as the Michigan jurisprudence examination.

In the United States, the field of pharmacy is currently growing and the job outlook is quite good. The employment of pharmacists is expected to grow due to the increasing size of the elderly population and its need for and greater use of medications.

For more information you can write to the following organizations:

American Association of Colleges of Pharmacy
1426 Prince Street
Alexandria, VA 22314

National Association of Boards of Pharmacy
700 Busse Highway
Park Ridge, IL 60068

SECTION 5 EXERCISES

The following exercises use the skills you have learned throughout this workbook. Assume that you have completed your requirements for becoming a pharmacist and you have decided to pursue a career as a retail pharmacy owner in your home community. Remember, your neighbors are counting on you to be helpful and accurate as their family pharmacist and to provide them with quality healthcare-related products at a fair price.

In your pharmacy you sell a particular brand of multivitamin which comes in three different sizes:

60 tablets	**$7.20**
120 tablets	**$13.20**
250 tablets	**$25.00.**

1. Find the unit price for the 60-tablet bottle.

Answer: _____

2. Find the unit price for the 120-tablet bottle.

Answer: _____

3. Find the unit price for the 250-tablet bottle.

Answer: _____

Suppose you purchased the 120 tablet bottles in boxes of 12 bottles for $110.88.

4. Find the markup rate based on cost for the 120-tablet bottle.

Answer: _____

5. Find the markup rate based on selling price for the 120-tablet bottle.

Answer: _____

While taking inventory, you noticed that you have been selling the 120-tablet bottles very quickly but the other two sizes are not selling as well. In order to increase the sales on the other two sizes, you advertise a sale in the daily newspaper:

"Multivitamin Special"

60 tablets	**Buy one, get 50% off the second bottle.**
250 tablets	**10% off**

6. Find the unit price on sale if you buy two of the 60-tablet bottles.

Answer: _____

7. Find the unit price on sale for the 250-tablet bottle.

Answer: _____

8. During the sale, a customer asks you which size is the best buy. What do you tell the customer?

_____

_____

_____

_____

_____

_____

One day, a customer from out of town came into your pharmacy in Erie, PA. This customer needed a refill on her prescription, but since she was from Los Angeles and did not originally fill her prescription at your pharmacy, you had to make a long-distance call to her doctor to confirm the prescription. Your pharmacy subscribes to Company A (see Table 4) for long distance. The telephone call was made on Tuesday at 2:37 p.m., and it lasted for 12 minutes.

9. What did this long-distance call to her doctor cost?

Answer: _____

10. If this prescription sells for $18.00 for 30 capsules, find the unit price per capsule.

Answer: _____

11. The medication in this prescription (see Exercise 10) cost you $39.00 per 100 capsules. Find the markup for the bottle of 30 capsules.

Answer: _____

12. Find the markup rate based on selling price and the markup rate based on cost for this prescription.

Based on selling price: _____

Based on cost: _____

It is the end of the month and you are paying the bills for your store. Find the amount you owe for each of the following utilities.

13. **Electricity:** Use the following declining-block rate schedule to determine the amount you owe to the electric company if you used 2256 kwh during this month. [**Note:** the following rate schedule has been simplified. In addition to the declining–block rate schedule shown below, there is a "demand charge." A demand charge is incurred by the business if electricity use exceeds a certain level every fifteen minutes (or whatever length of time is set by the electric company.) A computer reads the electric meter after each block of time and determines if the business exceeded the demand limit. If so, a charge is incurred. This particular electric company allows the business to exceed the limit five times for free. Beyond that, it charges $10.47 each time the limit is exceeded. For ease of calculation, this charge has been left out of the schedule. Keep in mind, though, that this could easily add up!]

    A. Base Rates

0–2000 kwh	$0.07130 per kwh
2001–4000 kwh	$0.03390 per kwh
4001–6000 kwh	$0.3100 per kwh

    B. Basic Monthly Service Charge $7.58

    C. Fuel-Cost Adjustment $0.009727 per kwh

    D. 6% State Tax on entire bill

Total Electric Bill: _____

14. Gas: Use the following declining-block rate schedule to determine the amount you owe to the gas company if you used 15,325 cubic feet of gas during this month. [**Note:** The rates quoted in this particular schedule are based on the "small volume commercial" rates. This is where the business uses less than 250,000 cubic feet of gas per year. If usage exceeds this level, there is a higher basic monthly service charge and slightly lower rates per cubic foot of gas.]

    A. Base Rates

        0–5000 cubic feet $0.0069661 per cubic foot
        above 5000 cubic feet $0.0067941 per cubic foot

    B. Basic Monthly Service Charge $16.25

    C. Surcharge $0.0002 per cubic foot

    D. 6% State Tax on entire bill

Total Gas Bill: _____

15. Local telephone service: Find the total amount owed to the local telephone company for the month if your business has the following telephone services.

Three telephone lines: One dedicated line to the pharmacy and two lines to the front end of the store. Each telephone line costs $23.29 per month.

Special features: The two front–end lines have a service called "roll-over" in which the second available line will ring if the first one is busy. This service costs $2.95 per month for each line involved in the roll-over. The line to the pharmacy does not have the roll-over option, but does have a voice mailbox, which costs $10.95 per month, and call waiting which costs $3.75 per month.

Taxes: There is a state sales tax of 6% applied to the total local bill.

Total Telephone Bill: _____

Solutions to "Try one!" Exercises

SECTION 1

Page 4

$$\text{Unit Price} = \frac{\text{Total Price}}{\text{Total Units}} = \frac{\$8.82}{56 \text{ oz}} = \$0.1575 = 15.75\cent \text{ per ounce.}$$

Page 5

$$32 \text{ oz: Unit Price} = \frac{\$1.69}{32 \text{ oz}} \approx \$0.0528 = 5.28\cent \text{ per ounce,}$$

$$64 \text{ oz: Unit Price} = \frac{\$2.79}{64 \text{ oz}} \approx \$0.0436 = 4.36\cent \text{ per ounce.}$$
Therefore, the 64–ounce carton is the better buy.

Page 7

Two 12.5–ounce bottles is the same as 25 ounces, so the
$$\text{Unit Price} = \frac{\$8.38}{25 \text{ oz}} = \$0.3352 = 33.52\cent \text{ per ounce.}$$

Six 4–ounce bottles is the same as 24 ounces, so the
$$\text{Unit Price} = \frac{\$9.54}{24 \text{ oz}} \approx \$0.3975 = 39.75\cent \text{ per ounce.}$$

Therefore, the 12.5 ounce bottles are the better buy.

Page 8

For the name brand tea bags, the $\text{Unit Price} = \dfrac{\$2.89}{100 \text{ bags}} = \$0.0289$ per bag.

Annual Cost = (365)(3)($0.0289) = $31.6455.

For the store brand tea bags, the $\text{Unit Price} = \dfrac{\$2.09}{100 \text{ bags}} = \$0.0209$ per bag.

Annual Cost = (365)(3)($0.0209) = $22.8855.

So the savings per year is $31.6455 − $22.8855 = $8.76.

Page 11

The larger container is 1 lb, 12 oz = 16 oz + 12 oz = 28 oz. If we choose the ounce as the basic unit of comparison, the unit price for the larger container is Unit Price $= \dfrac{\$3.29}{28 \text{ oz}} = \$0.1175 = 11.75$¢ per ounce. The unit price for the smaller container is Unit Price $= \dfrac{\$1.99}{14 \text{ oz}} \approx \$0.1421 = 14.21$¢ per ounce. Therefore, the larger container is more economical.

Page 13

We can choose the liter as the unit for comparison.

2–liter bottle: Unit Price $= \dfrac{\$1.59}{2 \text{ L}} = \$0.7950$ per liter.

20-ounce bottle: Total Units = 20 oz $\approx$ (20)(0.02957 L) = 0.5914 L, so the Unit Price $\approx \dfrac{\$0.79}{0.5914 \text{ L}} \approx \$1.3358$ per liter.

Therefore, the 2-liter bottle has the smaller unit price.

SECTION 2

Page 28

$M = S - C = \$1,040.00 - \$650.00 = \$390.00.$

Page 29

$S = C + M = \$125.00 + \$54.95 = \$179.95.$

Page 30

$C = S - M = \$22,495.00 - \$2,137.00 = \$20,358.00.$

Page 32

$R = \dfrac{M}{C} = \dfrac{\$54.95}{\$125.00} = 0.4396 \approx 44.0\%.$

$S = C + M = \$125.00 + \$54.95 = \$179.95,$
so $r = \dfrac{M}{S} = \dfrac{\$54.95}{\$179.95} \approx 0.3054 \approx 30.5\%.$

Page 35

a. $r = 40\% = 0.40$ and $C = \$47.70.$

So, $S = \dfrac{C}{1 - r} = \dfrac{\$47.70}{1 - 0.40} = \dfrac{\$47.70}{0.60} = \$79.50.$

b. $M = RC = (0.40)(\$47.70) = \$19.08.$

Page 36

$S = \$17,650.00$ and $r = 9\% = 0.09$.

So, $M = rS = (0.09)(\$17,650.00) = \$1,588.50$ and the cost to the retailer is

$C = S - M = \$17,650.00 - \$1,588.50 = \$16,061.50$.

Page 37

$S = \$219.95$ and $R = 130\% = 1.30$. So, $C = \dfrac{S}{1 + R} = \dfrac{\$219.95}{1 + 1.30} \approx \$95.63$.

SECTION 3

Page 50

$D = L - S = \$799.95 - \$679.96 = \$119.99$.

$r = \dfrac{D}{L} = \dfrac{\$119.99}{\$799.95} \approx 0.1500 = 15.0\%$.

Page 52

Since $D = L - S = \$162.50 - \$125.00 = \$37.50$, we have

$r = \dfrac{D}{L} = \dfrac{\$37.50}{\$162.50} \approx 0.2308 \approx 23.1\%$ as the implied discount rate.

Since $D = L - S = \$130.00 - \$125.00 = \$5.00$, we have

$r = \dfrac{D}{L} = \dfrac{\$5.00}{\$130.00} \approx 0.03846 \approx 3.8\%$ as the actual discount rate.

Page 54

Since $D = rL = (0.15)(\$14.98) \approx \$2.25$, we have

$S = L - D = \$14.98 - \$2.25 = \$12.73$.

Page 55

Since $S = \$119.96$ and $r = 25\% = 0.25$, we have

$L = \dfrac{S}{1 - r} = \dfrac{\$119.96}{1 - 0.25} \approx \$159.95$.

Page 56

Since $L = \$650.00$ and $r = 45\% = 0.45$, we have

$D = rL = (0.45)(\$650.00) = \$292.50$.

Page 57

The price for the six nights $= (6)(\$89.50) = \$537.00$.

The price for seven nights $= (7)(\$89.50) = \$626.50$, and

if you stay seven nights the discount is $D = rL = (0.10)(\$626.50) = \$62.65$.

Therefore, the sale price for the seven nights is

$S = L - D = \$626.50 - \$62.65 = \$563.85$. This means that the seventh

night in the hotel would only cost $\$563.85 - \$537.00 = \$26.85$.

SECTION 4

Page 69

Total local charges = three phone line charges + voice mailbox charge, so the

Total charges TC = 3($15.80) + $6.50 = $47.40 + $6.50 = $53.90.

Total Bill = TC + Tax + Surcharge = TC + (TC)(0.03) + (TC)(0.0019)
$$= \$53.90 + \$1.617 + \$0.10241 \approx \$55.62.$$

Page 72

a. Company A: 6:00 p.m. falls under the Evening rates and the per minute charge to Atlanta, GA is $0.17. Therefore, the cost for the call would be (15)($0.17) = $2.55.
Company B: 6:00 p.m. falls under the Weekday rates and the per minute charge is $0.25. Therefore, the cost for the call would be (15)($0.25) = $3.75. So, at 6:00 p.m., Company A would cost less by $3.75 − $2.55 = $1.20.

b. Company A: 7:30 p.m. falls under the Evening rates and the per minute charge to Atlanta, GA is $0.17. Therefore, the cost for the call would be (15)($0.17) = $2.55.
Company B: 7:30 p.m. falls under the Night/Weekend rates and the per minute charge is $0.10. Therefore, the cost for the call would be (15)($0.10) = $1.50. So, at 7:30 p.m., Company B would cost less by $2.55 − $1.50 = $1.05.

Page 76

a. Watt–hours = (# bulbs)(# watts/bulb)(# hours/day)(# days)
$$= (1)(35)(24)(30) = 25,200 \text{ watt–hours.}$$

$$\frac{25,200 \text{ watt–hours}}{1000 \text{ watt–hours per kwh}} = 25.2 \text{ kwh.}$$ At 6¢ per kwh, they spend

(25.2)($0.06) = $1.512 ≈ $1.51 per month.

b. They spent $6.48 per month using two 75–watt bulbs and now they spend $1.51 per month, so their savings is $6.48 − $1.51 = $4.97.

Page 78

BR = (600)($0.04906) + (335)($0.03754) = $29.436 + $12.5759
$$= \$42.0119 \approx \$42.01.$$

MSC = $11.00.

FCA = (935)($0.00391) = $3.65585 ≈ $3.66 (credit).

Total Bill = BR + MSC − FCA = $42.01 + $11.00 − $3.66 = $49.35.

Page 80

$BR = (8000)(\$0.0058354) \approx \$46.68,\ S = (8000)(\$0.0001351) \approx \$1.08,$
$MSC = \$11.35.$

$\text{Tax} = (BR + S + MSC)(5\%) = (\$46.68 + \$1.08 + \$11.35)(0.05) \approx \$2.96.$

$\text{Total Bill} = BR + S + MSC + \text{Tax} = \$46.68 + \$1.08 + \$11.35 + \$2.96$
$\qquad = \$62.07.$

Page 82

$BR = (700)(\$0.0675) + (350)(\$0.0785) = \$47.25 + \$27.475 \approx \$74.73,$

$S = (3\%)(BR) = (0.03)(\$74.73) \approx \$2.24,\ MSC = \$7.50.$

$FCA = (1050)(\$0.0125) \approx \$13.13 \text{ (charge)}.$

$\text{Total Bill} = BR + S + MSC + FCA = \$74.73 + \$2.24 + \$7.50 + \$13.13$
$\qquad = \$97.60.$

Page 84

$BR = (800)(\$0.06753) + (175)(\$0.04782) = \$54.024 + \$8.3685 = \$62.3925$
$\qquad \approx \$62.39,$

$MSC = \$7.50,\ FCA = (975)(\$0.01229) = \$11.98275 \approx \$11.98 \text{ (charge)}.$

$\text{Total Bill} = BR + MSC + FCA = \$62.39 + \$7.50 + \$11.98 = \$81.87.$

Answers to Odd-Numbered Exercises

SECTION 1 (pages 16–25)

1. 6.19¢ per ounce

3. 4.54¢ per ounce

5. $1.80 per pound

7. $1.09 per quart

9. $3.92 per quart

11. $1.68 per liter

13. 10–pound: 27.90¢ per pound. 5–pound: 31.80¢ per pound.
The 10–pound sack is the better buy.

15. 16–ounce: 11.81¢ per ounce. 12–ounce: 11.58¢ per ounce.
6–ounce: 16.50¢ per ounce. The 12–ounce can is the best buy.

17. $1\frac{1}{4}$–pound: 6.75¢ per ounce. 10–ounce: 8.90¢ per ounce.
The $1\frac{1}{4}$–pound container is the better buy.

19. 1.89 liter: $0.4180 per liter. 946–milliliter: $0.5391 per liter. 3.79–liter:
$0.3140 per liter. The 3.79–liter container is the best buy.

21. 2–liter: $0.0220 per ounce. 8–pint: $0.0171 per ounce.
The 8–pint pack is the better buy.

23. 5–pound: $0.3580 per pound. 10–pound: $0.3450 per pound.
25–pound: $0.3380 per pound. The 25–pound bag is the best buy.

25. 5–gallon: $0.89 per quart. 24–quart case: $0.865 per quart.
The 24–quart case is the better buy.

27. a. $26.52 saved per year.

b. There is no actual savings in driving to the farm to buy milk.

29. $5.20 saved per year.

SECTION 2 (pages 42–47)

1. $M = \$22.98$, $R \approx 85.2\%$, $r \approx 46.0\%$.

3. $S = \$151.95$, $R \approx 68.9\%$, $r \approx 40.8\%$.

5. $C = \$18,082.00$, $R \approx 9.9\%$, $r \approx 9.0\%$.

7. $M = \$1,351.50$, $C = \$2,898.50$, $R \approx 46.6\%$.

9. $C \approx \$29.97$, $M = \$24.42$, $r = 44.9\%$.

11. $M \approx \$91.99$, $S = \$199.96$, $r = 46.0\%$.

13. $S \approx \$665.45$. $R \approx 81.8\%$.   15. $M = \$7,800.00$ per year.

17. $S = \$255.36$.   19. $C \approx \$13,709.17$.

21. average markup rate based on cost $\approx 76.5\%$.

SECTION 3 (pages 61–65)

1. $D = \$9.20$, $r = 20.0\%$.   3. $D = \$2.10$, $r \approx 19.4\%$.

5. $S = \$294.73$, $r \approx 15.8\%$.   7. $D \approx \$13.99$, $S = \$55.98$.

9. $D = \$56.70$, $S = \$132.30$.   11. $L \approx \$1,016.77$, $D = \$167.77$.

13. $L = \$15.87$, $r \approx 31.4\%$.

15. Catalog Showroom: $D = \$115.03$, $r \approx 33.3\%$.

   Mail Order Catalog: $D = \$42.87$, $r \approx 12.4\%$.

17. Mail Order Catalog: $S = \$51.68$. Local Store: $S = \$47.99$.

   The local store is the better bargain.

19. First Reduction: $S = \$32.63$. Second Reduction: $D \approx \$8.16$,

   Second reduction sale price $= \$24.47$,

   Discount rate based on original list price $\approx 50.0\%$.

SECTION 4   (pages 88–97)

1. $1.04   **3.** $0.51   **5.** $3.75

7. $5.00   **9.** Savings: $87.36   **11.** $43.68

13. $30.09   **15.** Cheaper to use Company B with no additional discounts.

17. $26.40   **19.** $45.54   **21.** $55.91

23. $87.78   **25.** $23.81   **27.** $135.03

29. a. $93.90

   b. July has the greater bill by $11.42.

SECTION 5   (pages 102–109)

1. $0.12   **3.** $0.10   **5.** 30.0%

7. $0.09   **9.** $3.60   **11.** $6.30

13. $191.65   **15.** $95.90